To: Tony & Angela

THE LAST MILE: CONVERSATIONS WITH DICK GREGORY

SHELIA P. MOSES

BOOKS ALSO BY SHELIA P. MOSES

Dark Girls

Callus on My Soul: A Memoir with Dick Gregory

The Legend of Buddy Bush

The Return of Buddy Bush

I, Dred Scott

The Baptism

Sallie Gal and the Wall-a-kee-Man

Joseph

Joseph's Grace

The Sittin' Up

Project Success: The Right Thing for the Right Reason

I'm a Grady Baby

A Price Was Paid, The History of W.S.Creecy High School

One More River To Cross

So They Burned The Black Churches

COPYRIGHT

Published by

Braxton House Publishing Company

3213 Duke Street, #112, Alexandria, Virginia 22314

shelia@braxtonhousepublishing.com

Printed in the United States of America

First Printing 2019

ISBN: 9781731588937

Visit mosesbooks.org for more information or to order a copy.

For Dick Gregory

"The two most powerful forces on this earth are the black woman and the black church."

Dick Gregory

FOREWORD

Richard "Dick" Claxton Gregory was a comedian, civil rights activist, nutritionist, author, recording artist, actor, philosopher, and anti-drug crusader. He was also my greatest teacher, mentor and friend. I was his historian and keeper of the gate of the many moments of his life. I spent 25 years talking with, walking with, and listening to Dick Gregory.

After he died on August 19, 2017, I did only one interview and I wrote only one article because the wounds were so deep. Later I realized that his life stories should be heard by everyone, not for me to keep in my head and heart. I was there the day he took his last breath, but his words live on in hundreds of recordings that we made in long conversations from Atlanta to California, in restaurants and coffee shops, on trains and planes.

In *The Last Mile: Conversations with Dick Gregory*, I will share with you what he saw, heard, and experienced with people like Rosa Parks, John F. Kennedy, Martin Luther King, Jr., Malcolm X, John Lennon, Marvin Gaye, Bill Clinton, Dave Chappelle, Michael Jackson, Chris Rock, Paul Mooney, and Bill Cosby. It will provide moments in history that range from the day Dick met Medgar Evers in 1961 and became committed to the Civil Rights Movement, to his reactions to the slaying of Michael Brown five decades later. The book also will explore how Dick Gregory, at the age 81, felt about the childhood he first described to me for *Callus on My Soul: A Memoir*, published in 2000.

Dick Gregory was one of the funniest men in our history, one of the most political, and certainly one of the most controversial.

In the 1960s he brought a new perspective to the world of comedy and he opened many doors for black entertainers. He was an overweight, chain-smoking black man who became a household name for his outspoken and provocative humor. Once he achieved success in the entertainment world, he shifted gears and used his talents to help causes he believed in. He became even more known for his political commentary, civil and social rights activities, and for his work as an athlete/health diet guru. It was his stand against racism that virtually barred him from entertainment for many years.

As a social activist, Gregory was the nation's front-runner in and out of political seasons. He was fighting for causes he believed in whether he was running with a group or walking alone. While some leaders consult polls or focus groups to chart their course, he consulted his inner spirit—a reservoir of courage, wisdom, and direction. He was a prophetic voice—the nag who pestered our government to cease trampling on individual rights. His sense of justice led him from Louisiana to Iran, from Ireland to Detroit, always working for human rights.

Gregory also taught himself the basics of human nutrition in order to get to a healthy weight. He then developed and marketed "The Bahamian Diet." His work for better nutrition spanned the globe, with followers in urban American cities and in Third World countries using his nutritional supplements. He helped a number of the extremely obese (some topping 800 pounds) to regain normal lives. In addition, his nutrition research helped hunger strikers around the world advance their causes without risking their lives.

He was a living emblem for confidante in troubled times. Legends like Bobby Kennedy, Michael Jackson, John Lennon, and Marlon Brando sought his spiritually-rich counsel.

It's been over 50 years since the publication of Gregory's autobiography *Nigger*, followed by *Up From Nigger* in 1967. *Callus on My Soul* is more recent, but much has changed. The consistent force in those events that somehow touched our lives was Dick Gregory. He continued to inspire, protest, and call the powerful into account for their actions against the vulnerable until he died.

It is my hope that readers will finish this book having gained an important piece of history. It was not an easy task to summarize this extraordinary and vibrant man in just a few pages but I can say that I know that he is pleased with my work because it is what he taught me.

THE LAST MILE: CONVERSATIONS WITH DICK GREGORY

You often talk about poverty while growing up in St. Louis, Missouri. When did you realize your family was really poor?

When? Hell, it didn't take me long to figure that out. Let me tell you something about being poor. It is in your blood the rest of your life.

The only thing worse than being poor when I was growing up was watching my mother suffer. I mean she literally worked herself to death. She was so nice. Momma managed poverty like a champ not knowing that the stress would eventually kill her.

Her name was Lucille Jefferson before she married my daddy, Presley Gregory. She had an eighth-grade education and that made her a black woman in St. Louis, Missouri, with very few options. Like most of the women on North Taylor Street and our entire neighborhood, Momma was a maid. That was all she knew how to do. She worked for white folks and she liked it most of the time. I say she liked it because she never ever complained. Maybe she was just too kind to complain.

Momma left our small apartment before the sun rose almost every day and returned when it was dark. I rarely saw sunlight on her face. Just stop and think about that for a minute. The person you loved most in the world you rarely saw during the day. She worked seven days a week with one Sunday per month off.

My momma loved God, church and the people she worshipped with but they rarely saw her. That one Sunday she was off she would get us all dressed and we would go with her to church. On the Sundays Momma had to work we did not go. We said "to hell with that" and we stayed home.

So back to your question about poverty. Before I knew the definition of the word poverty I knew that not having money meant Momma had to work all the time. My sister Dolores, who is two years older than I am, grew up long before she was even a teenager. She grew up because she had to help Momma. We all helped but Dolores was in charge of us and the house when Momma was away. Momma could come home so tired but she would go in the kitchen and finish the dinner that Dolores started. Then no matter how late it was we would sit down and eat the little food we had together. No one would put a piece of bread in their mouth until she was sitting at the table. We loved her that much.

Momma would smile at us and ask us about school. I knew even as a boy that she was crying on the inside because she wanted to be home with us. Even on holidays she had to cook for white folks before she could prepare food for her own children. Sometimes she would pretend she was not hungry and eat just a little food so that there would be enough food for everyone.

All of this pain was enough to make her bitter, but not Momma. She was smiling with all that hurt in her heart.

You rarely mention your father. Tell me more about him.

It is really not a lot to tell. Not only did Momma spend most of her precious life working for white folks, she was married to a man who was not married to her. My daddy, whom we called Big Prez, only came home a few times a year. As time went on he started coming about once a year. At some point, I guess it was every two years because there is a two-year age difference between most of me and my siblings. Eventually he got tired pretending that he loved us and he just stopped coming, as if we didn't exist.

He probably would have come once a year for the rest of our lives if it was not for me. One night he got mad at Momma and slapped her in the kitchen. That was the end of Big Prez because I pulled a knife on him. Yes, he knew it would end badly if he kept coming around, but he was leaving anyway. He wanted a reason to never come back.

I didn't miss him when he stopped coming because I didn't really know him. What I knew I didn't like. When he was coming to St. Louis he stayed just long enough to get my momma pregnant. That alone was enough to make you mad but even then Momma kept on smiling. As a matter of fact, I never heard her say an unkind word about Big Prez.

So you combine poverty with a daddy that was never home and you get a callus on your soul that no amount of time will remove. As I got older, the thing I knew I did not want to be was so poor that I could not eat and not to have decent clothes on my back.

We had the clothes that Momma brought home from the white folks and we had the clothes the welfare department gave her twice a year. We called welfare "relief" back then. The social worker didn't care if the clothes fit, they gave Momma a box of clothes and we wore what was in the box. That was the only time we wore clothes that had not been worn by someone else.

I have a picture of me and my oldest brother Presley in T-shirts that were too big. Worse than that, I have an image in my head of the look on the faces of the children who teased us about our old worn clothes that were too big.

Now this is something very few people know. When I was in middle school I was sent to a school called Charles Turner Open Air Middle School. It was for children the Department of Social Services considered sick. Now my brother Garland had anemia so maybe he needed to go for a little while but they sent me and Presley because we were underweight. That's a bitch to be sent to a school for sick children and you are not sick. We were two healthy kids going to a school with sick children and they kept the windows open for fresh air as if that would cure us. I had never put that fact in a book before but it is out there now. My momma must have felt so helpless when they told her we would be enrolled at Turner and she knew we were in good health.

As a man, my prayer was for my wife and children to never experience that kind of hurt of watching others frown on them. That look of someone looking at you like you don't belong. That look of laughter and you know you are the joke.

Man, I think about all the times we got evicted on North Taylor Street. The landlord never told us we could not come back. He would just sit our furniture outside and we could not go back in until Momma came up with the money. Then the white landlord would stand there and listen to Momma beg him to let us back in. It was almost like he enjoyed it.

Not once was Big Prez there to help us. Not once! Yes, I was gone most of the time because we had lives to save during the Civil Rights Movement, but my children knew daddy was coming back. I am sure they all will tell you that I was gone a lot but they will never say we got hungry or we wondered if I was coming home.

No, no, no. I just didn't want them to know that pain. That is what poverty is. Poverty is pain.

If all the children in your neighborhood were born poor, why do you think you were teased so much?

That's a good question but I don't know the real answer. I believe we had two things against us. The minority of the children on North Taylor Street were poor but most of them had a daddy in the house. So kids were not just teasing us about raggedy clothes. They could not wait to say "You ain't got no daddy," or "Richard, where's your daddy?" I mean, they had no mercy on us. It was worse for me and my brother Presley. We were the oldest boys so we were picked on the most.

One day I just made up my mind that I was going to turn the table on my so-called buddies. When a neighborhood kid said "Hey Richard, where's your daddy?" I said "My daddy with your momma." Everyone on the playground laughed and I did, too. Now I didn't know it then, but that is the day the magic started to happen. I realized that people can't laugh at you if you laugh, too. I realized that I could make pain my gain and I have been doing that for over 60 years now.

After I made all the children on North Taylor Street laugh one time, I wanted to do it again. Every day I would run to the playground and tell jokes. If there was no one at the playground, me, Presley, and our friend Boo would wait on people to show up. I would go home at night and stand in the mirror and tell my jokes to myself until Momma arrived for dinner.

The next day we would go to school and there would be a new set of children to tease us. We could not run home and tell Momma because she was at work. We could not tell Big Prez because he was not there.

You lost your mother when you were very young. How did that affect you?

Momma's death changed everything. She was my everything. She was my sisters' and brothers' everything. Momma was all we had. She was the only person that we knew loved us.

I remember the exact moment I learned she was dead. I was a freshman at Southern Illinois University in Carbondale. When I wasn't away at a track meet or studying, I would go to the movies. I attended a college that would allow me to be their star on the track field but I was not allowed to sit with the white students to watch a movie.

So I was in the balcony when Coach Lingle got the call about Momma. When he didn't find me in the dorm, he knew exactly where I was.

The words "Your mother is dead, Richard" never left me. Sixty years later and I still remember the look on my coach's face. Far worse than poverty and bullies, the word "dead" hurt the most.

I remember going to the bus station but I don't remember much about the ride back to St. Louis. I was heartbroken that Momma was dead at 49 years old from heart failure, diabetes, and the lack of health care.

It is the same reason millions of black folks still die every year.

When I arrived in St. Louis everything was a daze. I don't remember how I got to North Taylor Street. What I remember is walking in that apartment for the first time in my life knowing that my mother would not be coming home. I will never forget the look on the faces of my sisters and brothers. It was a look of confusion.

Dolores must have been 20 or 21 when Momma died. She was married and lived nearby. She somehow pulled herself together and started making funeral plans. She told my younger siblings, Pauline and Ronald, not to cry. She met with the women from Momma's church and they arranged the funeral.

I remember white folks coming to our house. White folks didn't come to that neighborhood but they came in a hurry and left in a hurry to bring food when Momma died. They showed up at Momma's funeral and talked to us like they cared about us and our Momma.

After the funeral we went back to North Taylor Street. I didn't even spend the night. I got on the next bus back to Carbondale and never lived in St. Louis again.

Before I left, Dolores told me that she was taking my younger siblings, Ronald and Pauline, to live with her. They were still in school and they needed a mother. That is what she became to them and the rest of the Gregory family. Garland didn't go to live with our sister. He was only 16 but he had started working and he actually had enough money to live in a boarding house until he went to the Air Force.

Presley was in the Navy but he made it home for Momma's funeral.

Dolores had her own children but she opened her home to me and my brothers to come there whenever we wanted to. So the few times that I returned to St. Louis when I was in college I went to Dolores' house for home. My sister became our lifeline and I still feel the same way about her. We call her Dee. The only other woman on this earth I had that kind of respect for was my mother until I met my wife.

Speaking of your wife, do you think that it was fair that you are away from her most of the time?

Now you know better than to ask me a question like that. I am not away from home because I want to be away. In the beginning I was hustling as a comedian to feed my family. I was trying to make it during a time when we were far from welcome in the comedy world. When I did become famous … that fame came with a price. Long trips and lots of nights in a hotel became a norm for me. My family was not

included in my life on the road. Lil was and she is still not a tagalong-type woman. When I need her she is there but she is not the woman you will find sitting in a hotel waiting for me to come back.

Listen, when I married Lil, I thought I was marrying her because she was pregnant. I got married and went to Dolores with my bride. We were living in Chicago at the time. I was chasing my dreams and I was never at home. I took my bride to live with Dolores until the baby arrived. I left Lil there and she had my daughter Michelle on the floor alone while everyone was at work.

Dolores talked so much trash to me and I didn't say a word. I eventually sent for my family and thank God I did. Lil was and is the best mother ever. She has the love for our children that our momma had for us. I started to see her in a whole new light. There was nothing Lil would not do for me. There was nothing she would not do for her children and that is still true today.

She stood by me while I was following my dreams to become a comedian but then the movement called.

Once I started to march and give up gigs for the movement Lil joined me to march and went to jail if she had to. I mean this woman would come out with her babies on her hips, in her belly—you name it.

There have only been three women in my life that I know for sure love me. That's Lucille Gregory, Dolores Gregory and my wife Lil. Now my baby sister and my daughters love me but those three took it to a different level.

These three women cry when I cry, hurt when I hurt. So when people ask me about being away from Lil ... they don't know her at all. Yes, we were married to each other but we were also married to the movement. Lillian Gregory didn't march as Dick Gregory's wife. She is a woman of the movement ... so I am never really away from her.

You were a very wealthy man. Why did you trade everything for the movement?

I didn't join the movement. The movement joined me. I thought I was the happiest black man on earth when I made it big as a comedian. Within a matter of months, I went from having my wife give birth on my sister's kitchen floor to being the highest-paid black comedian on the planet.

I had the best wife a man could ask for and a family that loved me. We were free from poverty and that was new for me. Nice car, nice home, nothing was off limits to us. I was minding my own business when Medgar Evers, who was the field secretary for the Mississippi branch of the NAACP, called me. I wish I could remember the date but I know it was 1961.

It was not my first time marching. I had gone to marches before as Dick Gregory the comedian. But all of that was about to change. It was something about Medgar's voice that was unsettling. Before I got on the plane I sat down and talked with Lil. I told her I felt damage that I had never felt before. I could not put my finger on it but I knew Mississippi was not going to be easy. I told Lil that the movement would have to come first if I went to Jackson with Medgar. She didn't say a word that would stop me and I didn't want her to.

When I arrived in Mississippi I expected to see all the people I heard folks in St. Louis talk negative about, but that is not what I found. The first thing that happened that surprised me was Medgar didn't send someone to pick me up. He was waiting for me at the gate when the plane landed. He was that kind of guy. We talked all the way to his office. I kept wondering why he was not afraid. From the moment I met him I could see death all around him.

When we arrived at his office I saw the people that the news stations didn't show. They were having a meeting and preparing for the rally. Yes, there were people there who could not spell their name but there were also black doctors and teachers. The other thing that threw me was the fact the NAACP office was on Lynch Street. None of that bothered Medgar. I tried to joke about the street called Lynch as we drove from his office to the rally but Mississippi was no laughing matter. It was straight-out evil and you could feel it in the air.

I was on the program to speak at the rally along with the Roy Wilkins but nothing we said topped what an old man that was also on program had to say.

He told this incredible story of how he had gone to jail for killing a white man. This white guy tried to burn his house down because the old man was helping people in Jackson to register to vote. If Medgar and the national branch of the NAACP had not hired him a lawyer, white folks would have killed him or he would have spent the rest of his life in jail. The story about him going to jail was only half of the story. The other half was too painful to listen to. He was a 75-year-old man who got married at 17 to a girl who was 13 years old at the time. They had never spent a night apart. His wife died of a broken heart the second night he spent in prison.

I was messed up after that but the night was not over. Medgar had a way of making sure you got the point. Just in case the old man didn't wake me the hell up, he introduced me to a black woman named Leona Smith. Medgar told me that Miss Smith was Clyde Kennard's mother. Neither name meant anything to me but I listened to Medgar tell their the story. It turned out that her son, who was a paratrooper in the Korean War, was in prison. His dad died in 1959 and Clyde returned home to help his mother. He also enrolled in Mississippi Southern College and pissed a lot of white folks off. What is now the University of Southern Mississippi had no black students at the time and all hell broke loose.

While he was away at school white folks gave a black teen a five-pound bag of stolen chicken feed to plant on Clyde's farm. A few days later the sheriff showed up at Clyde's house. He was arrested and sentenced to seven years in Parchman State Penitentiary. Did you hear what I said? They did not send this young man to the county jail. Instead, they sent him to one of the worse prison systems in the country. If that was not bad enough, Clyde had cancer. Not only was Medgar trying to help him gain his freedom he was pressing the prison to give Clyde the medical attention he needed.

I left Mississippi a changed man. There was nothing I could do to help the old man whose wife died but I wanted to help Clyde. I talked about him everywhere I went. I would open my show talking about this young man.

At the time I was friends with Irv Kupcinet, who was writing for the Chicago Sun-Times. Irv did some research and found out everything I told him was true. When the story ran in the newspaper, Mississippi was exposed for their racism once again. He embarrassed the state of Mississippi so bad they transferred Clyde to a state hospital, but it was too late. He died on July 4, 1963. So when you ask me about trading in my wealth for the movement, you have to understand what I saw in Mississippi. There was no turning back.

When you talk about Medgar you speak in a different tone than when you speak about other civil rights leaders. Why is that?

Medgar is the man who changed my life. There is one person or one incident that will change you forever. Medgar was that person. Listening to the story about the old man and Clyde's mother are the incidents that changed me. On top of that, Medgar became my friend. We were brothers. What else can I add to that?

My drive was money and fame until Medgar called me. I thought my personal responsibilities were only to take care of my wife and children. I didn't know that it was my duty to help children around the world. Medgar taught me that and he taught me the meaning of sacrifice. When I met him I saw something I had never seen in a man before. He was willing to lay down his life, even if it meant leaving his own wife and children.

You know there was a difference between Medgar and other leaders in my eyes. No disrespect to Dr. King and men like Malcolm X, but they always had protection. No one could stop them from being assassinated in the end but they did not fight and die alone. Man, Medgar was alone most of the time.

So back to your question. I get to Jackson in 1961 and Medgar is at the airport to pick me up. He drove himself around until the very night he died. He walked in and out of the NAACP office alone. To and from meetings alone.

Now here is the catch. He knew they were going to kill him. He didn't know when and he definitely didn't know who, but Medgar knew. He was that guy in the 23rd Psalm: Yea, though I walk through the valley of the shadow of death.

I often think about the last few times I saw him. We were at a rally when he walked up to me and whispered in my ear.

"Greg, call home."

"I will call later," I told him.

"No, call now."

Then he looked at me and said, "Your son is dead. Call home."

So I call Lil and got on the next flight to Chicago. Our first-born son, Richard Jr. had died in his sleep from what they called crib death back then.

When I arrived in Chicago I went straight to the house that was filled with people who were trying to comfort Lil. I don't remember everyone but John and Eunice Johnson from *Ebony Magazine* were there. I remember them the most because they were not there for a story, they were busy helping Lil with the funeral arrangements and making sure she was okay.

That was the first and only time in our 60 years together I saw Lillian Gregory broken. Even with a broken heart, I left her a few days after the funeral and went back to Mississippi. I had to go because we had made a commitment to all the children, not just Richard Jr.

I will never regret going to back to Mississippi. If I had not gone I would have never seen Medgar alive again. After the march he drove me to the airport and we talked along the way. He knew that death was near and I did, too. Before I left, I turned to Medgar at the airport and said "It would have been an honor to die with you brother."

He did not say a word.

Death traveled to Mississippi before I could return. On June 12, 1963, while I performed at the Hungry I Club in San Francisco, a coward named Byron De La Beckwith was waiting in the bushes across from Medgar's house. He was waiting to murder Medgar while his wife and children were in the house. They were watching television. Not only were they watching television, they were watching President John F. Kennedy give a speech. With a rifle that you use to kill deer, Beckwith pulled the trigger and shot Medgar in the back. I don't know how he did it but Medgar pulled himself up with a bullet in his back and crawled to the door. His wife, Myrlie ran to the door. They told me that Medgar insisted that they sit him up in the ambulance as they rushed him to the hospital.

"Sit me up," he said.

Now "turn me loose."

I was so moved when I heard that he wanted to sit up before he died. He wanted to sit up because Medgar was not a man that would die laying down.

Did you look at the Civil Rights Movement differently after Medgar died?

Well, his death took away all of my fears. There was a time I was marching as Dick Gregory the comedian. I was going for one day and going straight back to work. All of that changed when Medgar died. He lit a fire inside of me that will never go out.

I was not there for Medgar's last breath but I was determined to be there for the men and women he left behind. That meant I was about to sacrifice everything that I had worked for.

I could no longer go to rallies based on free time from my comedy gigs. The gigs were now scheduled around what I had to do for the movement. Then I made a move that some celebrities thought made me a crazy man. I started to flat out cancel engagements so that I could not miss rallies and marches. The comedian they started to call to replace me was Bill Cosby.

I didn't care that they were calling Bill. The calls that I was interested in were those from SCLC, SNCC, the NAACP, and anyone in the movement.

All of this was a direct result of Medgar's leadership. I can never see another man in the light I saw Medgar.

The same year that Medgar was murdered, four little girls were murdered in Birmingham, Alabama. Did you attend their funeral?

Yes. There was nothing on the planet that was going to stop me from going to that funeral.

If there was any place in America that was worse than Jackson, Mississippi, during the 1960s, it was Birmingham. I had been thrown in jail numerous times and watched them mistreat our children with dogs and fire hoses as we tried to peacefully protest.

I was going back and forth between Jackson and Birmingham the summer of 1963. I had been pushed by a police officer before but I had never been beaten. That all changed one night when I was in jail with little children. Bull Connor sent some of his men to the jail to take the children away so we started pulling them back inside.   Man, they grabbed me out of that cell and beat the hell out of me. I am telling you this because I want people to understand that our children were in danger long before they bombed that church.

When I received the call that they had bombed Sixteenth Street Baptist Church I was horrified but not surprised. To understand the evil that happened that Sunday morning you have to understand the black church during the movement. Most hotels would not rent us rooms and some people were afraid to let us stay or have meetings in their homes, so the church became our safe haven. In May 1963, the Children's Crusade was organized in Birmingham. Sixteenth Street Baptist Church opened their doors to us over and over again for our meetings. When Dr. King, Ralph Abernathy and other leaders came to town, Sixteenth Street opened their doors to them for SCLC meetings.

If you asked me, I would say that two evils killed those little girls. One, white folks were mad about them opening the church for our meetings. The second one had nothing to do with Birmingham or any church in America. White folks were angry about the success of the March on Washington that happened on August 28, 1963.

So late in the midnight hour on September 14, 1963, a man named Robert Chambliss and other KKK members put a bomb under the steps at the church. They didn't know or care that it was Youth Sunday and little girls and boys were scheduled to be on program. As the girls looked in the mirror and probably straightened out their dresses and fixed their hair one more time … a bomb went off. Within minutes Carol Denise McNair, Addie Mae Collins, Carole Robertson and Cynthia Wesley were all dead.

I went to the funeral and watched them carry the bodies of the three little girls into the church. Carole Robertson's parents made the decision to have her funeral the day before at another church. I stood outside the church and thought about my own children. What it would feel like for them to die a violent death like the little girls endured. I had lost my son but he died in his sleep. I hope he was not in pain.

We really didn't know the full story of what happened to the girls and their families until Spike Lee released the documentary *Four Little Girls*. As much as I disliked the movie Spike directed about Malcolm X, he did a damn good job exposing what happened in Birmingham.

Speaking of losing our youth during the movement, can you tell me more about the role you played in recovering the bodies of freedom riders Mickey Schwerner, Andrew Goodman and James Chaney?

What I did when those young men went missing is left out of 95 percent of the articles and books written about them. I did what a man and a father was supposed to do, but here is what happened. I was in Russia protesting the murder of a black student at Lumumba University. He allegedly was dating a white girl and was found dead in the snow.

I left Russia immediately when a reporter from the United Press International told me that Schwerner, Goodman and Chaney were all missing. The two white guys and one black were investigating a church burning and the beating of some of their members. So on June 16, 1964, they drive to the scene of the arson and they got stopped on the way back to where they were staying. They were arrested and charged in Philadelphia, Mississippi. Deputy Sheriff Cecil Price waited until 10:30 that night to release them. Of course they were walking into a death trap.

Along with John Lewis and James Farmer, I met with Deputy Price and Sheriff Rainey. The meeting was a waste of time because I realized immediately that we were talking to the men who committed the murders.

As we were leaving I told James Farmer that we had to come up with a reward and that was the only way we would ever find their bodies. It was no doubt in my mind that they were dead. CORE did not have the money and neither did any other organization within the movement.

I called Hugh Hefner immediately and told him that I needed twenty-five thousand dollars as an advance against my gigs scheduled at his club. He didn't ask me one question. He sent the money to Lil immediately.

Once the reward was announced, a man contacted me and sent me a tape and a map of what happened to the boys and the location of their bodies. I turned it over to Bobby Kennedy. I have always considered Bobby a friend to me and the movement but I was a little pissed because the FBI announced a thirty-thousand dollar reward the next day. The appearance was that the larger reward resulted in the bodies being located and the truth was they already knew.

So on August 4, 1964, the FBI dug up the bodies in a dam on Old Jolly Farm outside of Philadelphia, Mississippi. The other horrible thing that happened was Lyndon Johnson selected that very day to bomb North Vietnam for an earlier attack on the United States. His press conference overshadowed the fact that the boys were found. The men who sent me the tape never claimed the money and I never checked to see if the FBI paid him.

Now listen to this. The parents of Schwerner and Chaney wanted the boys to be buried side by side in Mississippi. But the very state that murdered them would not allow them to be buried together because of the color of their skin. Tragic!

Speaking of the March on Washington, how did you feel that day?

August 28, 1963, was a day that nobody in this country will forget. Now there might be white folks that would say it was not a big deal but they know that is not true.

There were a lot of things going through my head during the March on Washington. I kept my eye on A. Phillip Randolph because you want to talk about having a dream. It was A. Phillip who came up with the idea to march on Washington in the 1940s. It would take almost 30 years for the march to happen, but he planted the seed for the historic day. Then there is Bayard Rustin, who was the mastermind behind scheduling everyone who spoke that day. Not just the speakers but every meeting, every step taken until we went home that night.

A lot of people spoke that day including me, but nothing was like listening to Dr. King. People call the speech "I Have A Dream," but it should be "America's Bad Check." The most important words that King said that day were related to the 100th anniversary of the Emancipation Proclamation. He said that America had written black folks a bad check. Then he spelled out all the things in the proclamation that should apply to black folks but none of those things were happening. Now folks don't remember that, but it is what he said.

Also, the "I Have A Dream" speech was not a new speech. He had given the exact speech before. What happened at the march was the great Mahalia Jackson was sitting behind

Martin and said, "Tell them about the dream Martin, tell them about the dream." He clearly could hear Mahalia talking to him and Dr. King let out what almost sounded like a roar. As you know the rest is history.

Another important thing that happened at the March on Washington was the speech that John Lewis did not give. John came armed with a speech and a question that asked "Which side is the federal government on?"

So if you look at some of the pictures from that day, there is an interesting picture of John, James Forman and Joyce Ladner sitting behind the Lincoln Monument. Now they were not talking about what they were going to order for lunch. They were rewriting John's speech. I later learned that the only reason John agreed to change his speech was because A. Phillip Randolph asked him to.

People today love John Lewis and rightfully so. He had and has some of the Medgar Evers spirit in him. He is fearless. Man, when Donald Trump said something negative about John Lewis, folks went crazy. Now John didn't say much. He has nothing to prove. He left his blood in the soil of the South too many times for folks to debate his loyalty to all of us.

He had a right to speak at the March on Washington, and in my opinion he had the right to ask any question he wanted to ask. No matter what was said, there was very little joy after the March on Washington because two weeks later four little girls were dead.

It was around 1963 when you became friends with Malcolm X. What was the difference between your relationship with Malcolm X and Medgar Evers?

Oh, it was a big difference. I was not always friends with Malcolm. Malcolm was "a say it like you mean it" guy. So when he first heard that I had joined Dr. King and others to march, Malcolm made a public statement and said, "What other organization has comedians like Dick Gregory as their leader?"

People rushed to tell me what he had said. I was neither upset nor offended. I understood where he was coming from. Malcolm had been on the battlefield a long time. He was aware that some celebrities would march for one day just to get publicity. He was not going to let movie stars just walk in and tell him what time it was. You had to prove yourself to Malcolm.

So one night I was in New York to perform and Malcolm heard I was in town. He found out what hotel I was staying in and called me. "Dick Gregory, it's Brother Malcolm. Why don't you come down to the mosque?"

"I said. Okay ... send a driver to pick me up." I hung up.

Now this was during the time when things were really heating up for Malcolm. Some people were trying to distance themselves from him. He was not expecting me to say yes, so a few minutes later the phone rang again.

"You can't come to the mosque. I know you have a huge white following and this is not a good idea."

"Malcolm, you send the car. I will say a few words and then we will take a picture. After that you can print it on the cover of *Muhammad Speaks*."

I showed up at the rally and that night was the beginning of a friendship that would last until he took his last breath.

He actually called me the day before he died. I was performing at the Basin Street in New York.

My friends called me Greg and by then we were definitely friends and brothers.

"Hey Greg, I am speaking at the Audubon tomorrow night and I want you to come."

"No Malcolm, I love you. As a matter of fact, I love you so much that I don't want to be there when they kill you. I don't want them to get two for the price of one. If I come they will kill both of us. I already told Lil to book me a flight to Chicago. I will be back when they tell me you are gone."

Malcolm was totally silent.

"And Malcolm," I said, "I called Adam Clayton Powell and told him not to join you. If he shows up they will kill him, too."

I was walking through the airport in Chicago when someone came up to me and told me that Malcolm was dead. I did something I didn't do when Medgar died. I cried. That "a man ain't supposed to cry" is BS. I cried because once again a voice was silenced.

What was the tone of the movement after Malcolm X was murdered?

By 1965, we had lost, Medgar, Malcolm, Kennedy, and so many unknown men and women. I was kind of numb to the pain at that point. During that same time period they murdered Jimmie Lee Jackson in Alabama.

People talk about Selma and Bloody Sunday all the time but they leave out how and why it really started. There was a young man named Jimmie Lee Jackson who was shot during a peaceful protest in Marion, Alabama, on February 18, 1965. People were protesting because civil rights organizer James Orange had been arrested during a march earlier that week for the right to vote. Jimmie Lee saw an officer hitting his daddy and he was trying to stop him when he was gunned down by Alabama State Trooper James Bonard Fowler. Jimmie Lee died on February 26, 1965.

Several rallies after his murder is what sparked John Lewis, Hosea Williams, and others to march on the Edmund Pettus Bridge. They were beaten and ran over by horses on a day we now call Bloody Sunday. Many marches would follow until Lyndon Johnson signed the Voting Rights Bill. My point is, we lost so many men and women that are somewhat left out of the history book in a short period of time that there was no time to mourn.

People don't realize that you were shot in the leg a year after Malcolm X was killed. Why don't you talk about this incident more?

The people that don't know that I was shot in 1966 are the same people who don't know that James Orange and Jimmie Lee Jackson started the movement that led to the Voting Rights Bill being passed into law.

I am not concerned about what people know about me. I care that thousands of people lost their jobs during the movement because they tried to vote. People in rural areas that lived in what they called tenant houses and sharecropped were forced out of their homes in the middle of the night with no place to go.

I want people to know more than the fact Dick Gregory was shot in Watts. What was going on in Watts had to be stopped. The local people were not protesting. They were rioting for the right reason but they were also destroying their own homes. Dr. Martin Luther King taught me the difference between a riot and a protest. Listen, there are areas in places like Newark, New Jersey, Detroit and Watts that were never rebuilt after the 1960s riots.

When I arrived in Watts I started walking into the crowd telling people to go home. I wanted them to leave because cops were everywhere and they were ready to kill anyone in sight. Someone in the crowd shot me by accident. Well … I have always assumed it was an accident. If they wanted to kill me they would have done so and not put a bullet in my leg.

The next day the headlines read "Dick Gregory Shot in Watts." It should have read, "Hundreds lost their homes in fires during the riots."

Three years after Malcolm was killed, Dr. King was assassinated. How did you learn he was gone?

April 4, 1968, was definitely one of the darkest days of the Civil Rights Movement. It's one of those moments that you remember where you were, what you were doing, and how you felt. It's a moment you never forget.

I was in the back of a car going to speak at Hartnell College in Salinas, California when the news about Dr. King came on the radio. I asked the driver to turn up the volume. We listened in silence until we arrived at my hotel. I rushed to my hotel room and turned on the television and the radio. I went back and forth listening to both until it was time to leave for my speaking engagement. I did that so that I could hear every lie that was told. Today when something happens and you are near a television, always record what they say in the first day or two. That is what really happened. After that it will change a thousand times. Boy, I wish I had recorded what they said the night King died. Lies, lies and more lies would follow.

As an entertainer, the show had to go on. I walked on stage and the sorrow took over. The students were in tears. I talked for two hours.

Do you feel Dr. King and Malcolm X could have accomplished more if they had worked together?

I am not sure that was necessary. We needed a man like Malcolm as much as we needed Dr. King. Their different backgrounds spoke as loud as their beliefs. There were people who could not hear King but heard and understood Malcolm. That works both ways. These two men were from different worlds. Malcolm's father was murdered by a white mob when he was a child. He lost his mother at a young age just like I did and was sent to foster care until he finally went to live with his sister in Detroit.

So many things happened to Malcolm that we don't know about. On the other hand, Dr. King was a preacher's kid. The Kings were not rich but they were not poor. He went to college and became a preacher.

Dr. King and Malcolm's childhood shaped them just like my childhood shaped me. What they had in common came to pass in the end. Both men dedicated their lives to the movement. These two brothers simply didn't see things the same way. Malcolm thought that King was too easy on white folks and King was determined to remain nonviolent. They were not enemies by any means.

They had one meeting and we will never know what Malcolm and Dr. King said to each other. What happened in that meeting went with them to their graves.

You were a candidate for president of the United States of America when Dr. King was killed. Did you consider ending your campaign?

Absolutely not! I suspended my campaign for 30 days, but to end it all together was disrespectful to his legacy. The one thing I know that Dr. King wanted us to do was to keep going. He didn't want the fight for freedom to end with his life. I think we all became more determined after he died.

I was on the road when Dr. King was assassinated, so Lil met me in Atlanta. We went to the funeral and there were thousands of people lining the streets. When everything was over, Lil went home and I went back on the campaign trail.

I am sure no one thought I would win. Truth is, I didn't think I would win, but the bar was raised when I got 189,000 votes. In 2016 to only receive 189,000 votes is laughable, but it was not funny in 1968.

I wanted to show black folks what it looked like to have a candidate that looked like them. I wanted to put fear in the white men around this country who thought that black folks were afraid to run for the highest office in the land.

When Obama ran for president, black folks voted for him even if they didn't believe in some of what he stood for. When I ran for president, black folks were still afraid to vote, period, so they were definitely afraid to vote for a black man.

You see the difference?

Two years before your run for president of the United States you ran for mayor of Chicago. Why did you take on Mayor Richard Daley with his successful track record?

That's the reason I ran. Look, we had a man in power in one city for 21 years. Chicago had more ghettos than any place in the country and the school system was failing our children. My question for black folks in Chicago was, "What has he done for you?"

Daley wanted the press to believe that he was not fazed by me running but he was more concerned than he ever let on. I will never forget going to protest in front of his home. When we got there, a mob of white folks were waiting for us, chanting, "Two Four Six Eight We Don't Want To Integrate." When we would not leave, they turned the water hose on us. This is five years after Bull Connor turned the hose on us in Birmingham. Five years.

Sometimes you just have to get in the race. Sometimes you just have to say, "I might not win, but I will run as long and fast as I can. I will not quit until the last bell rings." That was my statement to Richard Daley and all the white folks in Chicago that tried to oppress us.

At what point did all the marching and campaigning take a toll on your lifestyle and that of your family?

My lifestyle changed the day Medgar Evers called me. The way my family would live changed that day. One phone call and everything changed.

People don't understand that the movement needed more than bodies marching down the street. The leaders needed airline tickets, hotel rooms and food. There were times when homeowners would kick the local civil rights participants out of their house just for marching or trying to vote. We felt it was only right to help them. There were times when we had to relocate people because they were afraid to stay in their hometown.

My lifestyle changed because I would give money to the movement before I would buy a new car or clothes. That was in the beginning. It got really deep when I realized that it was more than giving up a fancy suit. There were times I would do a gig and give the entire check to SCLC or the NAACP. That is nothing to brag about because there were lots of entertainers that gave money. Ossie Davis, Ruby Dee, Sidney Poitier, Harry Belafonte, Marlon Brando—I mean, I can name people all day long.

I was draining our bank accounts and Lillian Gregory never said a word. She never said, "What about me?" She never said, "What about the children?" She was not the wife of a soldier. She was and is a soldier.

If you had the opportunity to run for election again, would you?

Not at my age but running for mayor of Chicago changed my life because I met Dr. Alvenia Fulton. Dr. Fulton followed my every move in the press, so when I announced that I was running for mayor she sent an unsolicited container of funny-looking green salad to my campaign office. Now I knew the FBI was watching me and Daley was mad as hell with me, so I wasn't about to eat food from someone I didn't know, and that included Dr. Fulton. I threw the container in the trash can.

A few days later Dr. Fulton came to visit me. We shared a meal together. I figured if she was eating it I could, too. I just sat and listened to her talk about health and nutrition. After that she could stop by any time with a good healthy meal or she would send me a package. Within weeks I realized how much better I felt. That was the beginning of my journey to eating healthy.

Not only did I change the way I ate but Lil changed her diet and the way she cooked for our children. They were probably eating candy with their friends but not at my house. Today they all eat healthy and to my knowledge they are all in good health.

So in addition to showing black folks that we had a place at the table in any elections, I changed how I eat at my personal table.

You were away from your children for most of their lives. Do you feel they know you or that you really know them?

I didn't know them as children. I was on the road their entire life. When I was not marching, I was on my way to a march. When I was not entertaining, I was resting for a gig. When I came home I tried to be the best dad I could be but I had no training in that field. I don't think you can teach what you don't know.

I know them better as men and women because I am an old man now. I travel, but not as much. Two of my three sons and one of my daughters live here in D.C. When I am not on the road, I see them. I don't drive anymore and my sons do that for me. The one thing they didn't get to do when they were small was see me perform. Now they come to shows and we have dinner afterwards. I know more about their lives than I have ever known because I talk directly to them. In the past Lil kept me informed on everything they did in school or at work. The thing is you can't make up lost time.

Another thing is they can never have the relationship with me that they have with their mother. She has never been away from them other than to go to the hospital to have a baby or to march during the movement. Now listen to this: The longest she ever stayed away was when she was thrown in jail. The sheriff found out that Lil was my wife so they wanted to release her. She was pregnant and needed to be home, but she refused to leave unless they let all the women go. She stayed in jail for two whole weeks.

So other than staying in jail for children around the country for two weeks, she never stayed away from her own. For everything I was not for them as a father, she made up as a mother. Now that I look back, I guess Lil is a lot like my mother because she clearly never complained about me to our children, just like Momma never talked about Big Prez. In a very small way, I am like Big Prez because I was away all the time, too. The difference is...Big Prez never did. Kind of funny how well children will treat a daddy that never abandoned them.

After Big Prez left, you told me you reconnected with him years later. How did that happen?

Well I damn sho' did not go looking for him. Big Prez did what most of the people who didn't believe in me did after I became famous. He found me!

Lil, a few friends, and all of my siblings have always been with me. They believed in me and I had no problem giving them anything I had when the good times were rolling. But out of the blue, Big Prez called Dolores when I started to appear on television. I had not seen him since he walked out on us after slapping Momma. Ronald, Garland, Dolores, and Pauline saw him in St. Louis because he had gone there a time or two and he stopped by to visit them.

Big Prez was living in San Francisco with his new wife and children. I was wondering how he managed to live with a woman out there but could not live with us. I was scheduled to perform in San Francisco so I arranged to meet with him. He came to the show and we went to visit him afterwards.

I had no intention of ever seeing him or talking to him again after that one visit, but Lil and Michelle were with me. When we got home, Michelle looked at me and said, "Daddy, you don't like your daddy, do you?"

That bothered me because no matter what Big Prez did to me and Momma, I had become a part of a nonviolent movement that also taught us not to hate. I realized that my daughter saw my hate for him in my eyes.

Because of what Michelle said, I stayed in touch with Big Prez, but it was small talk. There was nothing to say. During my visit, I had also learned that when he left us for good, he moved a woman who lived down the street from us with him to California. At some point he ended their relationship and married the woman I met. In the end he treated his mistress the same way he treated Momma.

I didn't mean to change the subject from the campaign and the movement. So let me ask you more about what happened in 1968. After Dr. King's death and your campaign was over, why didn't you go home?

I didn't go home because the movement will never be over. Dr. King's death did not warrant me abandoning the people that were still out there fighting for civil and human rights. Regardless of the Voting Rights Bill, there were still people in the South afraid to vote. It was not time to go home. On top of all of that, people were still dying.

Three months after Dr. King died, they killed Bobby Kennedy. I knew John Kennedy, but he was not my friend. Bobby was my friend. He was the attorney general, but I could pick up the phone and call him. He was a good listener and he understood black people and our struggle. If there was a white guy out there that should be remembered for trying to help during the movement, it should be Bobby not John.

I don't have a lot of regrets but I do regret not being able to go to Bobby's funeral. I didn't go because I was in jail. In 1966, I was arrested for illegally fishing in Washington State. I had gone there because Marlon Brando called me. He had to cancel a speaking engagement and needed my help. He asked me if I could go and speak to a group of Indians in Washington State. After my speech, they came backstage and asked me if I would join them in a protest. The government had outlawed fishing with a net in Washington, which was their way of earning a living. I went with the Indians fishing and we were all arrested on the spot. I went to jail and stayed a few days. We fought the case for two years, but a few days before Bobby was murdered, I was sentenced to 90 days in the county jail.

Now I made up my mind that I would do the time without a fight because thousands of poor people had gone to jail with me over the years. I could get out first because I was a celebrity and they would stay for days and sometimes weeks.

I said all of that to say ... that the movement was not over in 1968. It is not over now. Think about the fact that it is 2016 and we are having the same conversations that we were having when I met you 25 years ago. The same conversations I had with writers and reporters 50 years ago. On top of that, black folks were afraid of the police then and they are afraid now. There is no expiration date on racism.

You still have a special relationship with many Indians? Do you think things are better for them in this country now?

Listen, the only people on the planet that have been treated worse than black folks are Indians. Look at their lives. The Indians came to America first, not Columbus with all his BS we were fed in school.

The Indians were forced off their land onto reservations. Now they can't live in peace on the reservations. I am still offended that we have billion-dollar teams with names like the Washington Redskins and the Atlanta Hawks. In the nation's capital, where the most powerful people in the world live, we have a team called Redskins with a logo of Indians on their helmets.

In history and all of my years living in D.C., I have never gone to a game and I never will. I don't even go near the stadium. Politicians, preachers and so-called civil rights leaders go to the games and sit there while the Redskins play ball. They have no shame.

Can you imagine a team called Blackface or Cracker?

Back to Dr. King. After his death, who did you feel should be the next leader of the movement?

There were a lot of people who made suggestions about who should become the next president of SCLC but I was satisfied with Ralph Abernathy. Ralph was a quiet man and he was not the speaker that Dr. King was, but no one else was either until Dr. William Barber came on the scene 50 years later.

I trusted Ralph and his ability to lead. No one other than Coretta knew Dr. King better than Ralph. He knew what Rev. King wanted for SCLC and the movement.

One day people will have to go back and reexamine Ralph's contributions to civil and human rights. His wife, Juanita and children were threatened over and over again just like the King family. Now go back and look at the picture of some of the marches. Not only was he marching his wife and children would come on the road and march from morning until night.

We knew that Ralph could not replace King, but he did a damn good job. It was not my job to try to take King's place, but I was always there when needed. I returned to the campaign trail as I told you earlier. After I lost the election, I started to focus on the other issue that bothered me and that was the war in Vietnam.

How did you feel about the Vietnam War?

First, people have to think about and admit the real reason Dr. King was assassinated. He had been a target since 1955 when he started supporting the boycott in Montgomery. There were thousands of times he could have been killed.

The white folks turned on Dr. King for real when he spoke out against the Vietnam War at the Riverside Church. Oh, don't leave this out—Dr. King's speech at Riverside titled "Beyond Vietnam" was on April 4, 1967. Yep … that's right, one year before King was assassinated.

On top of that he was planning the Poor People's March in Washington, D.C. This march was not just about black people. Poor included the white folks, too, so that was going to triple the amount of people that came to D.C. in 1963.

I thought about the Poor People's March and I decided to go back to Dr. Fulton to learn more about the effect of hunger and nutrition. I did this because I was planning to go on a hunger strike to protest the war in Vietnam. That was 50 years ago and I have been on over 100 hunger strikes since that time.

When did you start walking daily and running marathons?

While I was fasting to protest the war in Vietnam, I decided to run the Boston Marathon. You know, back then only white folks ran the marathon so I thought I would help break down that wall, too. My lifelong friend and publicist, Steve Gaffe, my coach from high school, Coach St. James, Dr. Fulton, and of course Lil went with me to Boston.

The Boston Marathon is 26 miles long. I made it to the 25th mile and it was over. My legs started to cramp and I fell to the sideline. That race was over but the seed was planted for many more. My falling at the 25th mile told me that my body was not ready and I went back to learning more from Dr. Fulton.

One of the things that I didn't hear the first time was the importance of water. Now I don't drink less than a gallon of water each day. Listen. Fasting, marathons, and anything to improve your health will not work without drinking water.

At what point did you decide to run from Chicago to Washington, D.C.?

The goal was to run from Chicago to Washington, D.C., to bring awareness to hunger in our nation.

There were so many people to help me from day one. I don't know who introduced us, but I met John Bellamy around that time. He worked fulltime at the United States Post Office but he also volunteered for the Society of Writers and Editors. So this guy takes a leave of absence from the post office and joins our team. He would drive ahead of me from city to city. When John arrived, he would make sure the press was covering the run and made sure they understood what our mission was.

Civil rights leaders whom I had been marching with for years heard about the run and called Lil. They wanted to join me along the way. Lil would tell them when I was going to be in a major city where they could fly in and join me. Rev. C.T. Vivian and Ralph Abernathy ran with me for a day.

The guy who came and helped us the most was Muhammad Ali. The press went crazy when they heard Ali was running across the country with me. Ali was brilliant with the press and he knew they would come and they did.

After Ali ran with me for just five miles, other celebrities started to join me. He made people aware of our cause. The truth was ... anything Ali did, other people wanted to do it.

After months of sore feet, talking to the press, and trying to finish that last mile, we made it to Washington, D.C. It was

August 4, 1974 when Andrew Young, Walter Fauntroy, Louis Stokes and people I didn't know joined me on the steps of the Capitol in Washington, D.C.

Now if you go back and try to find a picture of all of us on those steps, I doubt if you will find it. The press didn't show up because rumors were flying around town that Richard Nixon was going to resign over the Watergate scandal. He didn't resign until the 9th but no one was writing about anything except him and Watergate.

After 1,000 miles and thousands of dollars, history did not record the good we tried to do.

How did it make you feel to know that your entire race across was done in vain?

Vain? Who said the race was in vain? I said that the press didn't write about it.

To say it was in vain is the same as saying the entire Civil Rights Movement was in vain and it was not.

Every time we marched, ran or went to jail it made a difference to somebody or some cause. I was and I remain in a war that will never be over because I don't believe that racism will ever be over. How can something end that the people in power don't believe is wrong?

Do you think black people will ever recover from the brutal treatment during the Civil Rights Movement?

Black people cannot recover from the movement until we recover from slavery. We have to get really tired like Harriet Tubman did. You know people to this day really don't know why she started freeing slaves. It all started with a damn bag of sugar. She stole a bag of sugar and she was so frightened that she hid from her master for five days. He beat her and that is when she decided that she would run away one day and she did. The problem was her mama and daddy was too scared to go with her so she went alone.

Harriet lived in New Jersey and worked as a maid. Years went by before she went back for her mama and daddy. Then she went back and freed people in the South that she didn't even know. There are no records to confirm how many people she really freed. If the historians give her credit for freeing 500, that means she freed 1,000 slaves. Her face on the $20 bill is a great honor, but I need them to say it out loud.

Harriet Tubman was as brave as any man that ever lived on this earth. She risked her life to free our ancestors. Say that she was a spy during the Civil War because that is the truth.

The Yankees befriended her and helped her make it back and forth to the South to get information about the South. She was making trips with and without their help. I need historians to give her that credit.

When you give people like Harriet Tubman their dues and talk about all the slaves that didn't make it North, then and only then can we recover from 400 years of slavery. You have to talk about all the people that died along the way. Only then can we talk about recovery from the laws of Jim Crow and the movement.

You talk about Harriet Tubman a lot. What about Dred Scott and the Dred Scott Decision?

No ... that is the wrong question. The question should be: What about Harriet Scott? We know a lot of Dred Scott but very little about Harriet. The historians who tell the truth know that she was the one who talked her husband into suing for their freedom. She was attending Second African Baptist Church in St. Louis at the time. Her pastor, John Anderson, had helped other slaves with legal problems. She learned that if you had ever been taken into a free state you were not a slave.

It's all in writing. All you have to do is look at the original court documents. The paper read, "Harriett and Dred Scott." Not "Dred Scott" and that is no accident.

So Harriet goes to church, and her pastor schools her on how to get her freedom, her husband's freedom, and their children's. This is the cruel part. Their master, a woman named Irene Emerson Sanford, had rented them out to a family in St. Louis but Irene was living on her plantation called the California. That meant she didn't want or need them. She was so outraged about the lawsuit that she fought them in court for 11 years. When it was all said and done, folks who don't read or listen think that the Scotts were freed. What really happened was a judge named Roger Taney ruled against them in the Supreme Court, so the Scotts thought they would spend the rest of their lives as slaves. If it was not for the son of Dred's original master who bought and freed them, they would have never been freed.

What is just as tragic is that the Chief Justice of the Supreme Court who ruled against the Scott family picture is still hanging in the federal building in Washington, D.C. So when people are running around the country tearing down statues they should not forget the fact that Roger Taney's portrait is still in Washington, D.C., in the federal courthouse like he is some hero.

Why do you think the true stories about Dred Scott and other slaves are told incorrectly?

Why? You know why! Because we live in a racist society that has not changed since Dred Scott was freed in 1857. We don't know all we should know about his wife because we live in a sexist society. Listen, there are thousands of slaves that we have no way of knowing who they were, where they came from, or where they are buried. That is not the case with Dred Scott. It is all recorded when you trace the men who owned him.

It's not just slavery, it is the history of people of color, period, that is being told wrong or just left out of the history books. Think about the people in the movement that were murdered as late as 1970 and we don't even talk about them. When I say "we" that includes black folks.

Fannie Lou Hamer is another woman and civil rights leader that deserves as much credit as any man in the movement if you want to keep score.

Her parents had 20 children. That's twice as many as I have with Lil. Not only did she live in poverty most of her life, from her own mouth we know that she was married to an abusive man. Now here's when history gets really get crazy. Historians rarely talk about her role in the movement.

White folks give us one sentence for the history books and that is all we know. When people talk about Fannie Lou Hamer, they say, "I am sick and tired of being sick and tired." They don't know what she did when she went to the

Democratic Convention in 1964. She went to Atlantic City to help unseat Mississippi's white-only DNC Delegation. By the way, moments before she started talking, President Lyndon Johnson gave a silly press conference about nothing to divert attention from Fannie Lou Hamer.

Regardless of Johnson's trick, that was a defining moment in history.

Are there other women you feel should have received more credit for their role in the Civil Rights Movement?

Oh, God yes. There are hundreds of women, but most of them we don't know their names. Just off the top of my head I think about Mary McLeod Bethune. Even blacks folks know more about the fact that she was appointed as a national adviser to President Franklin D. Roosevelt than they know about her as an educator. Now don't forget the cabinet she was in was called the Black Cabinet.

People today talk about the fact their grandparents were slaves. Well, Dr. Bethune parents, Sam and Patsy, were slaves. She managed to learn to read and write while living on a rice and cotton farm in Sumter County, South Carolina, where she was born. Not only did she graduate high school but she went to college.

I often wonder how the 15th of 17 children made it to college while her parents still worked for the family who were once their master. I later learned that her parents bought a piece of land from their former master and worked the farm themselves. Dr. Bethune helped her mother with laundry and one day she was holding one of the white children's book. The child grabbed the book and told her she could not read. That was her driving force. She wanted to prove to herself and that little white girl that she could read and learn.

Not only did she learn to read but years later during her second marriage, she moved to Florida where she started a school for girls and one boy who was her son. That school is now Bethune Cookman University.

Almost 100 years later you have to think about the fact that she is responsible for thousands of young people receiving an education, including Dr. Dorothy Height.

Speaking of Dr. Dorothy Height, I know you had a close relationship with her. What do you think her true legacy will be 100 years from now?

Well, I would not say we were close. We were friends. Again, I have been close to three women in my entire life and they are Lucille, Dolores and Lillian Gregory. I started watching how dedicated Dr. Height was to the National Council of Negro Women Organization that Dr. Bethune started. She had been a student at Bethune-Cookman and a member of the organization.

Dr. Height spent the rest of her life mentoring women across the country. She had the ear of presidents, congressmen, and the respect of the world. Just when I thought women couldn't ask for a better leader, she started working to purchase the building they were renting at 633 Pennsylvania Avenue. It is the only building on the Hill owned by African Americans.

Celebrities around the world including Bill Cosby made donations. Her ability to pay off the mortgage on an $8 million building speaks volumes because she didn't have to sell pies to make it happen.

I know that Bill Cosby supported many causes. With all the good he did for the world his legacy is damaged now. How do you feel about his situation?

I can't say because there has not been a trial so I know what you know. I know what the public knows. People tell me a lot of stuff that is a secret to most people but not this time. Black folks aren't saying a word because they don't know.

What I do know is ... I have seven daughters, so I need it to not be true that he abused women. My relationship with Bill Cosby goes back almost 60 years. To see him in this situation is painful. No matter how painful it is, I can't support anyone who is abusive. I have no choice but to hold my judgment until we learn more.

Here's my relationship with Bill. People have no idea how he got his break in the comedy business. By 1961, agents and nightclubs had had enough of Dick Gregory marching and protesting. The next hot black comedian on the circuit was Bill Cosby, and that is how it happened.

Again, I will hold my opinion on his situation today until I have all the facts.

Who do you think is the most misunderstood black man in America?

I think we are all misunderstood. I say that because I didn't ask to be in the Civil Rights Movement. I didn't ask to get watered down with a fire hose in Birmingham or shot in Watts.

People think we enjoyed putting our lives on the line, so for that we are misunderstood. Me, Dr. King, Hosea Williams, all of us would have preferred to be home with our wife and children or earning a living to provide for them. We could not do that because we had a greater calling.

As far as me being misunderstood, there are people who still think I joined the movement for fame the way the press stated in the 1960s. Hell, I was the most famous black comedian in the country. Why would I risk my life for fame? I risk my life for your freedom, my children's freedom, and children around the world.

You often mention how you feel about the press trying to destroy Adam Clayton Powell. Do you feel his legacy has been forgotten?

Sure, they tried to destroy him. Here's a man who was born into wealth and could pass for white. As a matter of a fact, he enrolled and passed for white while he was a student at Colgate University. The call for him to lead was so strong that he stopped pretending and became one of the greatest leaders of his time.

I have to say I learned a lot from Adam. He was much older than I was when I met him. He was born in 1908. The same year Adam was born his father was ordained the minister of Abyssinian Baptist Church in Harlem. They had over 10,000 members before the word megachurch was ever written.

Adam could not stay away from his daddy's church any more than he wanted to continue to pass for white. He came home, enrolled in Columbia University where he received his master's degree, and worked for his dad at the church. Before people even knew his name outside of Harlem, Adam had a newspaper called the *People's Voice*.

Now this is when things got ugly for Adam. He ran and won for Congress in 1944 and remained in Congress in 1971. He got off to a rocky start with white folks when he wrote a bill stating that you could not receive federal funds and display racism. From that day until the day he died some of his own colleagues were out to get him.

In the end they said he was using federal dollars for personal trips and he lost his seat to Charles Rangel.

Today when I think about Adam, I still see him walking down the street in Harlem, speaking and preaching. I still see people coming out of their homes to walk with him, talk with him. I see them looking up to a man willing to die for them. That was Adam.

Do you think that Adam Clayton Powell was before his time?

Before his time? There were a lot of people before their time. We just don't know their names.

I will give you an example. Most people never heard of Claudette Colvin. She was the first woman to sit on a bus and refuse to get up, not Rosa Parks. Let me correct that. She was not a woman. She was a 15-year-old girl when she was arrested. People, including black folks, think that giving her the dues she deserve will take away from Rosa's legacy and that is not true. Here's what black folks have to do if no one else will. We as black folks have to open our mouths and say on March 2, 1955, Claudette Colvin was arrested because she refused to give up her seat on a bus in segregated Montgomery, Alabama. We have to add that this happened nine months before Rosa Parks was arrested.

On top of the fact that she has never received her any credit for her brave spirit, the people who do talk about her claim she was not selected to carry on this charge because she was pregnant. She became pregnant after the incident, so if you are going to basically leave a person out of American history, please don't lie on them.

One day, one day soon I hope, historians will go back and say that they were wrong. One day they will write her name down and say that she was a brave young lady. Rosa Parks was the mother of the movement and Claudette Colvin was the teenager of the movement because people are stuck on these titles.

The difference between the two women is very simple. Claudette did not get on that bus with a plan to be arrested and go to jail. Rosa worked for the NAACP and she went there to be arrested. There is nothing wrong with that. What is wrong is when we don't give Claudette credit for planting the seed.

Do you think Dr. King and others knew about Claudette Colvin?

Sure they knew! This was five years before I joined the movement. I don't think that anyone was trying to discredit this young lady. Desperate times call for desperate actions and they made to move fast. Like I told you, Rosa was not just any woman in Alabama. She was the secretary for the NAACP. She understood the movement and what to do if the police tried to force her off the bus. During the movement we had strategies that we used almost daily. The NAACP came up with one and it worked. Hell, we would still be on the back of the bus if that had not happened.

Now remember this was just a few months after Emmett Till was murdered and the national press was trying to sweep his murder under the rug. As a matter of a fact, they would have done just that if it were not for his mother, Mamie Till Mobley.

The fact that Claudette Colvin was not chosen to ignite the boycott was not a mistake. The big mistake is that sixties later people still don't know her name.

What would you like people to know about Mamie Till Mobley?

Listen to me. … Before Rosa Parks, there was a woman named Mamie Till Mobley. All she did was send her 14-year-old son to Mississippi for the summer like thousands of black folks did each year. She told him the rules and expected him to follow them. She told him not to bother white folks because she understood the evil of Mississippi. Emmett did what teens do and didn't follow the rules. He dared to look at a white woman.

Everybody in Money, Mississippi, knew that Carolyn Bryant lied when she told her husband and his half-brother that Emmett made a pass at her. Remember that she is still alive and admitted to Timothy Tyson, who is a professor at Duke, that she lied. I don't have time to read his book but I read the paper every day. He clearly stated that she told him that "Nothing that boy did deserved what they done to him." So the question for me in 2017 is why isn't she is jail. Her age does not matter to me. A boy died because Carolyn Bryant lied. People need to say that out loud.

This is what I do know. He was a 14-year-old baby that Roy Bryant and J.W. Milam beat all night long. I don't know how Emmett lived through two grown men beating him like that. When they were done, they blew his brains out.

Now here's where bravery comes in and here is where folks that don't read miss the story. The sheriff's office had put

Emmett Till in a coffin and they were getting ready to bury him in Mississippi. His mother stopped the burial and insisted that her son's body was returned to Chicago. She was smart and knew how to work the press to make sure her son's murder was not in vain. She gets dressed like she is going to church and goes to the train station. Now I know she was hurting and wanted to be there for her son but she was not playing with the authorities either. The picture of her standing at the train station is the saddest but bravest picture I have ever seen, but it also the boldest.

People including the undertaker in Chicago insisted that she have a closed-casket funeral and she said no. Not only did she view the body but she allowed everyone in Chicago to come and see him. These two men had turned this handsome little boy's face into something you see in a horror show. People screamed, fainted, and cried as they walked by his coffin.

If that was not enough to wake up this country, John Johnson, who owned *Ebony Magazine*, put Emmett's picture on the cover of *Jet Magazine* and this country was never the same.

A lot of black folks had been murdered over the years but no one had done what Mamie Till Mobley did to reveal their killer or killers. In addition to the damage done to little Emmett Till, what else do you think changed the mood of the country when he was killed?

I can tell you the other factor. It was not a thing or incident. It was a man named John H. Johnson.

To understand what he did when Emmett was murdered you have to understand John Johnson's background. This guy was so hungry for knowledge as a child that he enrolled himself in 8th grade a second time for a reason you would not believe. He was from Arkansas City, Arkansas, and they didn't have a high school for Negro children in the area where he lived. They made it clear that you would be working in a factory or on a farm as soon as your ass turned fourteen. So John repeated 8th grade so that he could stay in school. Somewhere during that time his father died and his mother remarried. They all moved to Chicago and John enrolled in high school.

He was the editor of the school newspaper and he graduated in 1936. Now that would have never happened if he had stayed in Arkansas.

Here is when God stepped in and gave us *Jet* and *Ebony Magazine*. John was a speaker at an Urban League dinner while in high school and a man named Harry Pace was in the audience. He thought John was brilliant and he gave him a job as editor of the Supreme Liberty Life Insurance Company.

John would write stories not only about the insurance company but the black folks who had policies with them.

He later came up with the idea to start his own magazine with $500 he got from his momma. Now she didn't just have $500 lying around. She used her furniture as security for the loan because she believed in her son.

John Johnson understood that subscriptions keep a magazine going so he asked all 3,000 policy holders at Supreme Liberty to subscribe to what he called *Negro Digest* in 1942.

His 3,000 subscribers turned into 50,000. Do you know how hard he worked to have 50,000 subscribers within one year? By 1945 he had a circulation of 2 million and he renamed the magazine *Ebony Magazine*. In 1951 his weekly magazine called *Jet* Magazine entered the universe.

John's mission was to get information about black folks to black folks and anyone else who wanted the truth about our community.

People don't talk about the fact he was the first black person in Chicago to own a broadcasting company. To make sure children were reading, he started *Ebony Jr.* and for a short period of time a magazine called *African American Stars*. Not only was he brilliant, he had a Lillian Gregory of his own named Eunice.

People talk about the Ebony Fashion Fair that she started in 1958 like it was only about clothes. No, no, no! This fashion show raised over $50 million for the United Negro College Fund.

When *Ebony Magazine* became an online magazine and *Jet* was shut down, black folks were looking crazy and wondering what happened. I will tell you what happened. Black folks didn't understand what John understood about subscriptions. We stopped subscribing and started getting our news from internet outlets. So black folks ... the man that started a magazine for you is the man that YOU let down. You let his legacy down. So there you have it. John Johnson is the other soldier in the Emmett Till story.

People don't give Mamie Till Mobley the credit she deserves but you have said the same thing about Paul Robeson so it's not sexism, it's racism.

No, it's both.

Here is a guy who graduated class valedictorian from Rutgers College and earned a law degree from Columbia University. He was an All-American football player, actor and singer. White folks loved him until he spoke out against racism in this country and started to criticize the government. It got really ugly when he expressed his sympathies for the Soviet Union and communism.

He was investigated during the McCarthyism era. When asked to recant some of his public statements he refused and the government took away his passport. Before that he was traveling the world performing.

Now the government never took away my passport but my own earnings were decreased for taking a stand against racism. Paul felt he had to stand up for what was right. He did small concerts for a while but sickness won and he basically went into seclusion with his family in Harlem. I never talk about this because he was such a private man at the end of his life, but I went to see Paul while he was living in Harlem. It was not easy to see him in bed so ill and frail. I remember that he had huge feet that were not under the cover. This giant of a man was reduced to very little flesh, bones and feet that reminded me of his long walk for justice.

Eventually he went to live with his family in Philadelphia and that is where he died. I don't have many heroes but Paul was one of them.

Let's talk about some of your celebrity friends that were not in the movement. Can we start with Marvin Gaye?

Marvin Gaye? Why do you think that Marvin was not a part of the movement? He was not out there marching with us but he was damn sho' singing about us. Have you ever listened to the lyrics to "What's Going On?" His message was very clear. In one song he sums up the movement by mentioning police brutality and war. You name it and you will find it in that song.

But to answer your question, I was very fond of Marvin. He came to me at a very difficult time in his life. He was having problems with his dad and he was battling a drug addiction. I don't have a lot of regrets but I regret my response to Marvin when he reached out to me a few days before his dad shot him.

I was with Marvin and I was trying to help him once again to detox from drugs. He didn't have any money with him and he said, "Go ask my money man, the white boy, to give you my money." I am not sure why he referred to him as the "white boy," but those were his words. When I went to the "white boy" things changed between me and Marvin.

The "white boy" said, "Marvin doesn't have the right to ask for money." I didn't say a word because I was mad at myself. I had money in my pocket and I should have just purchased what we needed. I went back to Marvin and went off.

"Why the hell did you humiliate me like that Marvin?"

"Sorry, man," Marvin said in the low voice he had when he was upset.

I left Marvin in the hotel and called Lil. I told her that I didn't want to talk to Marvin. If he called I told her not to tell me. Well, he did call. Over and over he called the days leading up to his death, and Lil didn't tell me.

I was out on the road on April 1, 1984. Lil could rarely catch me in the hotel unless it was late at night but she caught me that day. She said, "Marvin was just killed by his dad." I felt like I did when the coach told me Momma was dead. I was really hurt. To add to that pain, his road guy called me and said, "Greg, Marvin knew he was going to die." He kept saying, "If Greg don't get me out of this house my daddy is going to kill me."

His sister called Lil and asked me to call her. I was kind of shocked that they wanted me to do the eulogy. They knew I had turned Marvin away but his family also knew how much I loved my brother.

I think people are shocked that you were so close to John Lennon. How did that happen?

In my 81 years on this earth I have never sought out a celebrity for anything. John Lennon's camp reached out to me because he was battling a drug addiction just like Marvin Gaye. What usually happens is someone in their camp will convince them to get help. Managers knew they could trust me and they would call and ask me to meet with cats like John Lennon and Marvin Gaye.

By the time I met John and Yoko, I had developed Formula Four X and a new formula called Correction Connection. I don't remember the year, but it is all documented. He told me that John and Yoko were in a cave in Amsterdam drugged out. I was thinking, "a damn cave." Someone in his office sent me an airline ticket to Amsterdam. I spent weeks with them as we prayed and fasted together. They used the Correction Connection products and got clean. It was probably 10 years before I ran into one of his good friends who told me that John and Yoko both never used drugs again.

John Lennon getting clean meant more than giving the world good music again. It meant he could help others who really needed a man with that much power. He was already giving away millions of dollars to help support world peace. He started having sleep-ins all over the world so that he could invite the press and tell them what he was doing to help others. I often joined them on the road. We would meditate, pray, and then I would talk and they would listen.

Now here's something funny. If you look at the credits on his very famous album called *Give Peace a Chance*, you will see my name. I was there recording and singing along with them. I often think about what he could have done for the world if he had lived.

You spent a lot of time with the Jackson Family. How did you feel about losing Michael at such a young age?

Dr. King was murdered when he was only 39 years old, Malcolm was 40, and Medgar was 42. Michael was 50 years old when he died. Michael's life feels long after losing so many friends during the movement, but I was still hurt by his death. I knew Michael when he was a little boy. When he died, I thought about that little boy and how sad his life really was. Now understand I feel the same way about Michael that I feel about Bill Cosby. It is a problem for me if it is ever proven that he abused anyone.

This is how I feel about the Michael I did know. He was a brilliant man with no formal education. He never finished high school to my knowledge so I guess he got an at-home certificate or something like that. There was no entertainer like him. King of Pop, whatever you want to call him. No one could sing, dance, or handle a crowd like Michael.

In the early '90s, he reached out to me. He said he wanted to know what was going on in the world. He spent so much time on the road that he felt detached from the real world.

I went to visit him and we would sit for hours and he would ask me questions just like you are doing now. I would answer and sometimes he would just say a name.

Tell me about Malcolm X. Tell me about Dr. King. He wanted to know more.

When he went on trial, Michael was in worse shape than what you saw on television. His dad, Joe Jackson, called me and asked me to come to California. The day we were waiting for the verdict, Michael locked himself in his room and refused to come out. When I went to his room, I was shocked at the fear in his eyes. He hugged me and said, "I'm scared." I saw more than fear. I saw a very sick man. I know when a person is dehydrated.

"When is the last time you had water. Not soft drinks, etc. I am talking about water?"

"They are trying to poison me, Greg. I can't drink anything."

I could not believe it. He was a prisoner of his own fear.

"Have you had any food?"

"No," he said as he went back to bed.

I called one of my friends who had a special machine to test for dehydration. After we tested Michael, I convinced him to go down to San Francisco and check into a hospital. I didn't want to go by plane so his security team drove us down there. That was a dangerous move because the next day the doctor told me that if we had not checked Michael into the hospital he would have died in 24 hours.

When he was released, he did not go home. He went to my farm in Plymouth and stayed with me. From that point, he felt indebted to me. I would allow him to pay me for my services but he would try to overdo it and I would not allow that. I would tell him, "Look, take your money and go buy a new monkey or a lollipop." He thought that was so funny.

Was I sad when Michael died? Yes! I was sad because I don't believe the lie the press fed us about how he really died. This is what I know for sure. People loved Michael Jackson until he announced that he had purchased Associated Television.

At first people were like, "So what?" They thought he had purchased a cable station, but Associated Television owned the Beatles songbook. The songbook was valued at $47.5 million. When Michael died the songbook was worth $1 billion. The other thing that bothered the hell out of me was the fact that the Lloyd's of London had a $17.5 million insurance policy on Michael for the shows he was supposed to do in London. Not just shows, but 50 shows. Michael was that guy worth more dead than alive.

What about comedians? Do you have a favorite?

I don't have a favorite comedian but I like Dave Chappelle
and let me tell you why. He can do what we call flat-footed
comedy. A lot of comedians today can make videos, etc., but
he is old school and he can just stand on his feet and go for
hours. Not only is he telling good jokes, he is talking about
racism, politics, you name it.

I don't just like Dave. I respect him. Now it's not a lot of
money to some of these guys today because they are making
millions on top of millions, but in 2005 Dave Chappelle
walked away from his show on Comedy Central and a $50
million payout. He simply didn't like the terms of the
agreement and he walked out. I thought about how I walked
out from millions in the 1960s when I didn't agree with
racism in America. Yep, Dave Chappelle is my man!

What about female comedians?

You know who I really dig is Phyllis Stickney. Phyllis has never received the credit or the money she deserves for her talent. She is funny as hell and she is hip to the world and what is wrong with it.

It's amazing how much research she has done on comedians from my generation. When I run into Phyllis she can tell me 10 things about me in 10 minutes that I have not thought about in years.

Like so many female comedians, Phyllis has been overlooked by the mainstream media. That does not take away from her genius.

You told me a lot about celebrities that many people don't know. What are some of the things you think people don't know about you?

Hmmmm! I think very few people realize I was drafted into the Army. It's not something I talk about a lot because it was BS to me. I was in college when I was drafted. Even before I became a part of the movement I knew the Army was for white folks, not me. Why should I defend a country that I could not vote in?

Then I think about the 54th Massachusetts Infantry Regiment. Now the only thing that some folks know about them is what they saw in the movie *Glory*.

Don't think for one minute that the Union wanted black soldiers. They didn't have a choice. Abraham Lincoln's Civil War was headed into three years when a soldier named Lewis Hayden went to the governor of Massachusetts and convinced him to let freed slaves join the Union. The Fifty-Fourth was sent on one of the most dangerous missions in history. On that mission was one of Frederick Douglass's sons, a guy named Lewis Henry Douglass. They were trying to take over Fort Wagner in South Carolina. Who do you think they sent in to die? You got it. The Fifty-Fourth.

They did what I was not willing to do. Yes, I got kicked out of the army because I was not going to fight the white man's war. When the movement called, I was willing to die. I am still willing to die for my people.

Speaking of Abraham Lincoln, why do you think he is so admired by black people?

I don't think all black people admire or admired Lincoln. Those are your words not mine and you are supposed to be more hip than that. I taught you better. Here's the deal with Lincoln. History does not teach us that he was against slavery. The public and private school system taught us that lie.

For folks who read and understand the Civil War, they know what really happened. If you don't know let me hip you.

Lincoln was not a popular president with folks in the South. He was caught between saving the Union and how the hell he was going to pay for the war to continue. He went to all the banks in New York to try to borrow the money. Well the banks told him "yes" but they wanted to charge him 36 percent interest.

Lincoln came back to Washington and ordered the government to print new money instead of paying the 36 percent interest. So now he had money and not enough soldiers. Once again he was trying to save the Union. Go look in the history books. He said, "If I could save the Union without freeing any slaves, I would do it. And if I could save it by freeing some, and leave others alone, I would do that."

In no history book will you see the words "Slavery is wrong" from the mouth of Lincoln. When a man disagrees with something that he knows is wrong … they should say it out loud.

Dr. King was very clear when he said "Segregation is wrong." He did not say, "Segregation is wrong for SOME people." All I am saying is ... black folks have to carefully pick their heroes and stop passing lies to their children.

You don't feel that way about John Brown. Why do you feel it's necessary to go to Harpers Ferry every year?

I don't go once a year. I go three times a year. I go on my birthday, which is October 12th, and I go back on the 16th of October because that is the date of the raid. December 2, 1859, is the day they hung John Brown, so I go back and just pray. Now I say this about very few white folks but it applies to John Brown: "White is not a color, it's an attitude." Yes, he was born white but something happened to him during his lifetime that made him hate slavery as much as any black person that ever lived.

To understand John Brown you have to understand Harpers Ferry and why John Brown went there in the first place. He went to Harpers Ferry because that is where the government made bullets and military rifles. This place was so valuable to the government that they had four divisions of troops serving as security both night and day.

I don't know how they did it, but John Brown showed up at Harpers Ferry and wounded a large number of the men. The crazy part was he only had 24 men with him and only five were black. So here you had a man that was not only willing to die to end slavery but he sacrificed the life of two sons who were with him.

I will never say that it was right for John Brown to kill any of

the men at Harpers Ferry any more than I will say slavery was right. This is what was right: He wanted to end slavery.

There was no Civil Rights Movement for him to march and sing songs. He only knew war and that was what he used.

Sleep on this. John Brown's last words were: "The Negro will be freed and it would be the biggest bloodbath in the history of war." Sixteen months later we were in the Civil War.

Speaking of slavery, how did you feel about the way Hollywood treated Nate Parker regarding "The Birth of a Nation."?

Well, I don't know Nate Parker so I don't feel anyway about him and I didn't watch the movie. When I heard about it I knew that all hell would break loose. This brother had done a lot of research from what I read. He made a number of trips to Southampton, Virginia, to prepare for the role.

I think white folks were outraged at the thought of a black man making a movie about killing white people, but Parker had a bigger problem than Hollywood. He was accused of rape and that came up again when he decided to make a film about Nat Turner. So let me say this again about these guys accused of rape, assault and anything that violates another person. I will never defend them no matter who they are and that includes my sons. If any of what Nate is accused of is true then the courts should deal with it. I really don't want to speak on that but I can speak on what happened with Nat Turner.

When he was a little boy some white folks took a special interest in him and gave him a Bible. His master thought he was smarter than their other slaves but they had no problem selling him. After that they sold him and his momma. Years later he got married and they sold his wife.

I can't imagine Lil being sold away from me and that could very well have pushed him over the edge.

One might imagine that white folks didn't know that Nat Turner had learned to read that Bible. He started praying for a vision about what to do. On February 12, 1831, there was a solar eclipse and Nat saw that as a sign. After that he started planning the revolt for July 4th of that same year. He was sick on the 4th and saw that too as a sign that it was not time. In August the sun changed to a strange shade of green and blue and he was determined that was his sign.

On August 22, 1831 Nat Turner and 70 other slaves and freed men attacked and killed Joseph Travis and his family. Many people think that Travis was his master but that is incorrect. He was actually renting Nat Turner from his owner at the time of the raid. They went from house to house killing women, men, and children. It would take white folks almost two months to catch them, but they did on October 30th. On November 11, on what we now know as Veterans Day, they hung Nat Turner along with 55 men. Another 200 slaves were killed by white mobs across Virginia.

So, no, I am not surprised that they went after Nate Parker for trying to tell the story. They would do the same thing if someone tried to make a movie about John Brown. That's a hard pill for white folks to swallow.

We were talking about what people don't know about you before we started discussing slavery. Let's talk about aging. Do you think a lot about growing old?

No! I thought they would have killed me long before they killed Dr. King. I say that because I thought about death every day after they killed Medgar. I was not scared nor obsessed. I just thought that I would be next.

The Civil Rights Movement was dangerous. I was out there weekly and sometimes daily. They killed Medgar, Kennedy, Malcolm, and those four beautiful little girls, all before 1965. I didn't just think they were going to kill me, I thought they would kill all of us. So, no, I didn't think about getting old. When I turned 60, I thought God had played a joke on me. Seventy was shocking but this 80 thing is a bitch.

The thing about getting old is I got to see a part of the dream Dr. King talked about. I lived long enough to see a black president of the United States of America. On a personal note I have lived long enough to see my children become adults. Dr. King's children were young and Medgar's were even younger. Not only were Malcolm's children small but they saw their father's assassination. Growing old gives you time to be grateful and look back at all the things you didn't have to suffer through and all the things your children did not have to endure.

I have spent zero time wondering what people think about me and that includes my family.

I am too old to be trying to right any wrongs. I am not taking a survey on my life. To me there is still injustice going on in this world so that is my focus.

Sixty years have gone by and we still don't have anyone in jail for killing Emmett Till any more than for Michael Brown, who was just murdered in 2014. Think about that!

Before we close, what would you like to say about Michael Brown? I know that was personal for you because it happened in Ferguson and so close to St. Louis.

Well, the difference between Mike Brown and Emmett Till was we only had John Johnson and Mamie Till Mobley in 1955 to show and tell us what happen to Emmett Till.

Today we have the internet, black radio and young folks out here making speeches and creating organizations like Black Lives Matter. We don't know what words were exchanged between Mike Brown and that cop. This is what I know. I know that nothing he said justified a cop shooting him that many times. If the young man was a threat to him, one bullet in the knee would have stopped him. I need you to think about that.

What they did to Mike Brown you would not do to an animal. After they killed him he laid in the street for four hours. Where was the ambulance? If the cops left a white boy in the street for four hours, everybody from the mayor down could have lost their job.

This is what white folks were not counting on with black folks in Ferguson. They had no idea that they would rise from the ashes the way they did. Those black folks were not playing. This town is 70 percent black and 60 percent of them were in the streets protesting. They were not out there a few hours; they would be out there all day and all night long.

When the not guilty verdict came down, I was not surprised. What surprised me is white folks walking around in shock at our response. You got to realize that black folks are tired. They were not going to back down any more than Mamie Till Mobley did in 1955.

I went to Ferguson because I wanted to see if I could help. What I walked into was a situation that I had not seen since the night I got shot in Watts. I saw people willing to burn down their own homes before they take anything from this racist society.

I have never asked you this question before but what would you like your legacy to be?

I don't care and here's why. I don't think my legacy can be boxed into a book that you or anyone else wrote or will write about me. There is no movie or documentary that can tell my story. Only God and Lil Gregory know how I really live my life.

When I was out there on the battlefield marching, going to jail and watching little girls being buried, I never thought about what the end would be. I didn't think about what people would say the next day or 50 years later. This is what I need historians including you to get right. I need people to tell the truth about what happened to Emmett Till. I need people to get it right why Bloody Sunday really happened. John Lewis and Hosea Williams deserve their place in the history books for taking that ass whipping on that bridge. But while we tell their story don't leave out James Orange and Jimmie Lee Jackson. Don't forget Claudette Colvin when you talk about Alabama. Record the story of why Indians are still being mocked like they are mascots, not human beings.

What people say about Dick Gregory will not change the world. If the real historians tell the real truth about those brothers and sisters at the bottom of the Mississippi River that went missing during the movement, I will be satisfied.

I am proud of my work as an athlete, comedian, and actor, but what will it do for my great-great grandchildren one day? Now when they read that I was shot because I was trying to stop a riot I hope that will give them the courage to be brave. When they realize that I sat with Dr. King and talked about their freedom I feel that will help them to get involved in a worthy cause.

I am old now and this journey is almost over. I just want folks to tell the truth about what happened to my people and that was no damn joke.

ACKNOWLEDGEMENTS

This book is a labor of love. The long hours I spent with Dick Gregory were all worth it in the end. I feel it is important for people to know what Dick Gregory really said during our final interviews in 2015 and 2016. I am grateful to him for his wisdom over the years.

I want to also say thank you to Dick's siblings, whom I interviewed numerous times from 1994 until 2017. His brother Presley Jr. and his sister Dolores are gone to glory with Dick and their beloved mother, but they played a big part in my life for many years. Ronald, Garland and Pauline are still in St. Louis where Dick's journey started so long ago.

Thank you Mrs. Lillian Gregory for always being so kind, sharing and caring. You are everything your husband said you were.

It takes so much to get a book into the stores and the hands of readers. Editor Deborah Heard is as loyal as any person I have ever met.

I am grateful to my mother, Maless Moses, my siblings Barbara Moses Lucas, Johnny Moses, Scarlett Moses Spivey, Larry Moses, Leon Moses, Gayle Moses and Jackie Moses.

My sister- and brothers-in-LOVE, Ted Stewart, Iris Moses, James Lucas and Al Spivey, are the pieces of the puzzle to make our family even better. My nieces and nephews and their children make every book that I write worth more for generations to come.

Thank you all … and in the words of Dick Gregory, "God Bless You."

About the Author

National Book Award Finalist Shelia P. Moses started writing at age six and never stopped. After retiring from the Speakers Bureau—where she represented the likes of Bill Duke, Danny Glover, and Planet Hollywood—Moses started writing full-time. Since, 1994 she has written 19 books, including *The Legend of Buddy Bush*, which not only won her an NBA nomination, but the Coretta Scott King Honoree Award. The sequel *The Baptism* earned her an invitation to read for President George Bush at the National Book Festival. In 2000, she wrote Dick Gregory's memoir *Callus on My Soul* and executive produced his tribute at the Kennedy Center in Washington, D.C., the same year.

Her first contemporary novel, *Joseph*, was nominated for the NAACP Image Award in 2009. Her novel *The First Footer* will be released in the fall of 2019. Shelia is currently writing a book titled *Let The Church Say Amen*.

35206995R00066

Made in the USA
Middletown, DE
05 February 2019